SIDE HUSTLE SPARK

Igniting Income Streams in 45 Days

Dan Rooney

Table of Contents

INTRODUCTION

Dive into the illuminating pages of "Side Hustle Spark: Igniting Income Streams in 45 Days," a literary guide that stands as a beacon for those seeking to transform their financial landscapes. In an era where traditional career paths are evolving, this book emerges as a definitive manual for harnessing the power of side hustles.

Within these chapters lies a transformative 45-day journey, meticulously charted to navigate the intricate realm of supplementary income. From inception to execution, this guide offers a roadmap enriched with pragmatic advice, relatable anecdotes, and expert perspectives. Uncover the art of ideation, the science of planning, and the magic of monetizing your passions.

More than a mere how-to, "Side Hustle Spark" transcends the conventional narrative, delving into the psychology of success and the art of time management. With a spotlight on personal growth, financial empowerment, and fulfillment, this book encapsulates the essence of embracing entrepreneurial spirit within the bounds of a bustling life.

Whether you seek to bolster your financial stability, indulge your creative impulses, or embark on a new vocational trajectory, this literary endeavor promises to kindle flames of inspiration. Join us in reshaping your professional narrative, and let "Side Hustle Spark" be your guiding light toward a more prosperous and purposeful future.

CHAPTER ONE

The Side Hustle Mindset: Unlocking Opportunities in Today's Economy

In the landscape of modern economics, the concept of a traditional career has evolved. The once stable and linear paths have given way to a more dynamic and interconnected professional world. As the boundaries between work and personal life blur, individuals are increasingly seeking ways to diversify their income and find fulfillment beyond the confines of their 9-to-5 jobs. This quest for financial independence, creativity, and personal growth has propelled the rise of the side hustle—a term that not only represents an additional stream of income but also embodies a unique mindset.

The Economic Imperative of the Side Hustle

The importance of a side hustle in today's economy cannot be overstated. Traditional employment structures are shifting, and the idea of a lifelong, single career path is becoming obsolete. Automation, globalization, and technological advancements have transformed industries, leading to both new opportunities and unprecedented challenges. The gig economy, remote work revolution, and the democratization of entrepreneurship have empowered individuals to take charge of their financial destinies.

A side hustle serves as a proactive response to these changes. It offers a safety net during economic uncertainties, a means to experiment with alternative career paths, and a way to diversify income streams. Moreover, a side hustle can be a platform for turning passions into profits, allowing individuals to indulge in their creative pursuits while generating supplementary income.

Exploring the Psychological and Emotional Aspects

Embarking on a side hustle journey goes beyond the financial gains; it's a transformative experience that shapes one's mindset and emotions. The decision to start a side hustle is often driven by a desire for personal growth, self-discovery, and a sense of ownership. This shift in focus from just making money to personal development is a profound psychological change.

One of the primary psychological benefits of a side hustle is enhanced self-efficacy. As individuals navigate the complexities of managing their own venture, they develop a heightened sense of competence and control. Each successful milestone achieved—a product launch, a sale, positive customer feedback—reinforces their belief in their abilities. This newfound confidence often spills over into other areas of life, contributing to increased resilience and adaptability.

However, the journey is not without its emotional challenges. Balancing a side hustle with a full-time job and personal commitments can lead to feelings of overwhelm and stress. The fear of failure, imposter syndrome, and the pressure to perform can be mentally taxing. Thus, cultivating emotional intelligence and stress management techniques becomes crucial for maintaining a healthy balance between the demands of a side hustle and personal well-being.

Overcoming Self-Doubt and Fear of Failure

The path to a successful side hustle is paved with self-doubt and fear of failure. These emotions are intrinsic to any entrepreneurial endeavor, but they can also be harnessed as catalysts for growth. To overcome these hurdles, a mindset shift is paramount.

One such shift is reframing failure as a stepping stone to success. Every setback, mistake, or challenge is an opportunity to learn and improve.

Embracing a growth mindset allows side hustlers to see failures as valuable lessons rather than indicators of inadequacy. Additionally, setting realistic expectations is crucial. Recognizing that success rarely happens overnight and that setbacks are a natural part of the journey helps to mitigate feelings of disappointment.

Moreover, building a supportive community can significantly impact one's mindset. Surrounding oneself with like-minded individuals who understand the struggles and triumphs of the side hustle journey provides a sense of camaraderie and accountability. Sharing experiences and learning from others' stories reinforces the idea that challenges are universal and surmountable.

Conclusion: The Power of the Side Hustle Mindset

In conclusion, the side hustle mindset is more than a means to earn extra income—it's a transformative approach to life and work. The shifting economic landscape demands adaptability, creativity, and a proactive approach to career development. By embracing the side hustle mindset, individuals can harness their passions, build resilience in the face of challenges, and unlock their fullest potential.

The journey is not without its hurdles, but the rewards—both financial and personal—are immeasurable. Overcoming self-doubt and fear of failure through mindset shifts, embracing personal growth, and nurturing emotional well-being are all part of the package. As the side hustle becomes an increasingly integral part of modern livelihoods, developing the right mindset is the foundation upon which success is built. So, whether you're exploring a passion, testing a business idea, or seeking financial stability, remember that the power to ignite change and create meaningful income streams lies within the side hustle mindset.

CHAPTER TWO

Navigating the Idea Jungle: Unveiling Lucrative Side Hustle Concepts

In the landscape of contemporary entrepreneurship, the idea is the seed from which successful ventures germinate. The journey of nurturing an idea into a thriving side hustle is both exciting and daunting, akin to navigating through a dense and vibrant jungle. This chapter delves deep into the art and science of generating, evaluating, and selecting side hustle ideas, while also emphasizing the importance of aligning personal passions, skills, and market demand. Through a blend of practical techniques and illustrative case studies, aspiring side hustlers are empowered to venture into the idea jungle with confidence, emerging with concepts primed for success.

The Idea Generation Process

Effective techniques for generating side hustle ideas go beyond mere brainstorming; they involve a strategic approach to identifying unmet needs, gaps in the market, and areas where personal expertise can shine. Techniques such as mind mapping, problem-solving exercises, trend analysis, and creative inspiration journeys can all spark a flow of potential concepts.

One key approach is leveraging one's own life experiences. Personal challenges, hobbies, and interests often hold the seeds of viable side hustle ideas. A keen observation of daily routines can reveal pain points that could be addressed with innovative solutions. Moreover, staying attuned to emerging trends and cultural shifts opens doors to ideas that cater to evolving consumer demands.

The Art of Idea Evaluation

Generating ideas is merely the first step; evaluating their feasibility and potential is paramount. An effective evaluation process entails a blend of practicality and passion. Understanding the potential target audience, the scalability of the idea, and the resources required is crucial. A SWOT (Strengths, Weaknesses, Opportunities, Threats) analysis can provide a comprehensive overview of the idea's viability.

However, it's equally important to gauge personal enthusiasm. The sustainability of a side hustle is often tied to the founder's genuine interest and passion for the concept. A side hustle that aligns with one's values and interests has a higher likelihood of weathering challenges and thriving over the long term.

Aligning Passion, Skills, and Market Demand

The sweet spot of a successful side hustle lies at the intersection of passion, skills, and market demand. A side hustle that excites the entrepreneur, capitalizes on their strengths, and addresses a genuine need in the market has a higher chance of resonating with customers.

Understanding the target market is pivotal. Researching consumer behavior, preferences, and pain points can guide the refinement of an idea. Moreover, seeking feedback from potential customers at an early stage can offer valuable insights for improvement.

Case Studies: Learning from Success Stories

Case studies provide invaluable real-world insights into the process of transforming an idea into a lucrative side hustle. Examining successful ventures reveals patterns, strategies, and approaches that can be applied to new ideas.

Take, for example, the case of Sarah, a graphic designer who noticed a demand for customizable digital illustrations. By combining her artistic skills with the growing trend of personalization, she launched an online platform offering tailor-made digital art. Through strategic marketing and engaging social media content, she cultivated a loyal customer base and turned her passion into a profitable venture.

Another case study is Mark, a fitness enthusiast who identified a lack of accessible, home-based workout programs. Leveraging his background in fitness training, he created a subscription-based video platform offering a variety of workouts. By tapping into the increasing desire for convenient fitness solutions, Mark transformed his idea into a thriving side hustle that caters to a global audience.

Conclusion: Navigating the Idea Jungle with Confidence

In the journey of igniting a side hustle, the idea jungle is both exhilarating and challenging. The techniques explored in this chapter provide a compass to navigate through the dense foliage of possibilities. Generating and evaluating side hustle ideas requires a delicate balance of creativity, practicality, and personal resonance.

Aligning passion, skills, and market demand is the beacon that guides aspiring entrepreneurs toward fruitful ventures. As the case studies demonstrate, the transformation from idea to successful side hustle is not only possible but also achievable with the right strategies and mindset.

In the world of side hustles, the jungle teems with potential. By applying the techniques outlined in this chapter and drawing inspiration from real success stories, individuals can confidently traverse the landscape, emerging with side hustle concepts that are not only lucrative but also deeply fulfilling. The journey is unique for every explorer, but armed with the tools and insights offered here, anyone can venture forth and unearth the gems hidden within the idea jungle.

CHAPTER THREE

Crafting Your Side Hustle Blueprint: A Roadmap to Success

Every successful endeavor begins with a well-defined plan—a blueprint that outlines the path from concept to realization. The journey of creating a thriving side hustle is no exception. This chapter delves into the art and science of crafting a side hustle blueprint that not only clarifies your goals and strategies but also provides a detailed step-by-step roadmap for the crucial next 45 days. By setting realistic expectations and defining measurable success metrics, you'll be equipped to navigate the challenges and opportunities that arise along the way.

Clarifying Goals and Strategies

The first crucial step in crafting your side hustle blueprint is to clearly define your goals and strategies. Your goals serve as the destination toward which you're working, and your strategies are the routes you'll take to get there.

Begin by asking yourself: What do you want to achieve with your side hustle? Are you aiming for supplemental income, full-time entrepreneurship, or personal growth? Understanding your overarching objectives will shape every subsequent decision.

Equally important are the strategies you'll employ. These could encompass product development, marketing, networking, and more. Consider how you'll differentiate yourself from competitors and how you'll leverage your unique strengths and skills.

Creating a Step-by-Step Roadmap

Once your goals and strategies are in place, it's time to create a step-by-step roadmap. This roadmap serves as your detailed action plan, breaking down the journey into manageable tasks and milestones. A 45-day timeframe is ideal for this purpose, offering a balance between ambition and feasibility.

Start by identifying the critical tasks that need to be completed within this time frame. These could include market research, product development, branding, website setup, and initial marketing efforts. Break each task into smaller sub-tasks and assign deadlines to keep yourself on track.

Remember that flexibility is key. While a roadmap provides structure, the journey is dynamic. Be open to adjusting your plan as you encounter unexpected challenges or opportunities. Adaptability ensures that your blueprint remains relevant and effective.

Setting Realistic Expectations

One of the greatest pitfalls in the pursuit of a side hustle is setting unrealistic expectations. It's important to acknowledge that building a successful venture takes time, effort, and dedication. Unrealistic expectations can lead to frustration, burnout, and disappointment.

Set attainable milestones that reflect your current commitments and resources. Consider the time you can realistically dedicate to your side hustle alongside your primary job, family responsibilities, and personal well-being. Prioritize tasks and recognize that not everything needs to be done at once.

Defining Measurable Success Metrics

Success is often subjective, but it becomes tangible when you define measurable metrics. These metrics act as signposts, indicating progress and providing a sense of achievement.

Depending on your goals, success metrics could include the number of sales, website traffic, social media engagement, or customer testimonials.

Quantitative data offers insights into what's working and what requires adjustment. Regularly track these metrics to assess your progress and make informed decisions.

Case Study: Crafting a Side Hustle Blueprint in Action

To illustrate the process of crafting a side hustle blueprint, let's consider the case of Alex, a photography enthusiast aiming to establish a photography services side hustle.

Clarifying Goals and Strategies: Alex's goal is to generate supplemental income from his photography skills. His strategies include specializing in portrait photography, building an online portfolio, and using social media to showcase his work.

Creating a Step-by-Step Roadmap: Alex's 45-day roadmap includes tasks such as researching target demographics, setting up a professional website, creating a portfolio, and initiating a social media content plan.

Setting Realistic Expectations: Given his full-time job, Alex allocates evenings and weekends for his side hustle. He sets milestones that align with this schedule and recognizes that growth may be gradual.

Defining Measurable Success Metrics: Alex tracks website traffic, social media engagement, and the number of inquiries and bookings received. These metrics provide insights into his side hustle's performance and guide his marketing efforts.

Conclusion: Navigating Your Side Hustle with Precision

In the realm of side hustles, success doesn't occur by chance—it's the result of meticulous planning, strategic execution, and consistent effort. Crafting your side hustle blueprint empowers you with a roadmap that guides your journey, aligns your actions with your goals, and enables you to measure your progress.

Setting realistic expectations ensures that you approach your side hustle with a balanced perspective, avoiding burnout and disillusionment. By defining measurable success metrics, you're equipped to track your achievements and make informed decisions.

The case study of Alex highlights how a well-crafted blueprint can transform aspirations into reality.

Whether your goal is financial independence, creative expression, or personal growth, crafting your side hustle blueprint is your compass to navigate the terrain with precision. As you embark on this journey, remember that the blueprint is not just a static document—it's a living guide that evolves alongside your ambitions and dreams. With every step you take, you're one stride closer to turning your side hustle into a thriving reality.

CHAPTER FOUR

Launchpad: Transforming Ideas into Reality

The journey from a mere idea to a tangible, thriving product or service is a transformational one. This chapter serves as the launchpad for your side hustle, guiding you through the practical steps of bringing your concept to life. We'll delve into the intricacies of turning your idea into a tangible offering, exploring branding, prototyping, and initial marketing strategies. Additionally, we'll uncover quick and cost-effective methods to establish a strong online presence, ensuring your side hustle takes off on the right trajectory.

Turning Ideas into Tangible Offerings

Bringing an idea to life requires a systematic approach. Begin by refining your concept into a clear and well-defined product or service. Break down the offering into its key components, features, and benefits. This clarity not only helps you communicate your offering effectively but also guides subsequent decisions.

For tangible products, consider prototyping—a crucial step in the development process. Prototypes allow you to test functionality, identify potential flaws, and gather feedback before a full-scale launch. This iterative process ensures that your final product meets quality standards and customer expectations.

Exploring Branding Strategies

Branding is the heart and soul of your side hustle—it's what sets you apart from the competition and communicates your unique value to customers. Develop a brand identity that encompasses your business's personality, values, and mission. Your brand should resonate with your target audience, evoking emotions and building connections.

Select a memorable business name, design a captivating logo, and establish a consistent visual and verbal language. Your branding efforts should reflect the essence of your offering and the experience you aim to provide to customers.

Initiating Initial Marketing Strategies

Marketing is the bridge that connects your offering with your target audience. During the early stages of your side hustle, it's essential to generate buzz and interest. Begin by identifying your ideal customer—understand their preferences, pain points, and behaviors. Tailor your messaging to resonate with this audience, highlighting how your offering solves their problems or fulfills their desires.

Leverage social media platforms to create a presence and engage with potential customers. Share behind-the-scenes glimpses, teaser content, and engaging stories to build anticipation. Collaborate with influencers or micro-influencers who align with your brand to amplify your reach.

Quick and Cost-Effective Online Presence

In the digital age, establishing an online presence is vital for reaching a broader audience. However, building a website from scratch can be daunting. Thankfully, there are quick and cost-effective ways to create an online hub for your side hustle.

Consider using website builders that offer user-friendly templates and customization options. These platforms allow you to showcase your offering, share your story, and provide essential information to potential customers. Additionally, secure relevant social media handles to maintain consistency across platforms.

Case Study: A Real-Life Launchpad

To illustrate the process of bringing an idea to life, let's explore the case of Emily, an aspiring artisanal candle maker.

Turning Ideas into Tangible Offerings: Emily refines her idea of creating handcrafted, eco-friendly candles. She sources high-quality materials, including natural waxes and fragrances. After experimenting with various formulations, she develops a range of scented candles that align with her brand's ethos.

Exploring Branding Strategies: Emily develops a brand identity centered around sustainable living and self-care. She chooses the name "Green Glow Candles" and designs a logo that features nature-inspired elements. Her packaging is eco-friendly, reflecting her commitment to environmental responsibility.

Initiating Initial Marketing Strategies: Emily identifies her target audience—individuals who value eco-conscious products and appreciate the therapeutic benefits of scented candles. She creates engaging social media content, showcasing her candle-making process, sharing candle care tips, and offering glimpses of the ambiance her candles create.

Quick and Cost-Effective Online Presence: Emily uses a website builder to set up an online store. She includes vivid product images, detailed descriptions, and a section explaining her brand's story and mission. She links her social media profiles to her website, allowing customers to easily connect and explore her offerings.

Conclusion: Launching Your Side Hustle with Confidence

The journey of turning an idea into a tangible side hustle is marked by dedication, creativity, and strategic thinking. As you embark on this journey, remember that every step—from prototyping to branding to online presence—plays a crucial role in shaping your venture's success.

The case study of Emily showcases how these steps come together to create a cohesive and impactful launch. By refining your offering, creating a compelling brand, engaging in effective marketing strategies, and establishing a strong online presence, you're setting the stage for a successful launch.

As your side hustle takes flight, keep in mind that the launch is just the beginning. Building momentum, nurturing customer relationships, and continuously refining your offerings are all part of the ongoing journey. Armed with the insights from this chapter, you're well-equipped to navigate the launchpad with confidence, transforming your idea into a reality that resonates with customers and sets the foundation for future growth.

CHAPTER FIVE

Balancing Act: Navigating Time Management for Side Hustlers

In the intricate tapestry of modern life, time is a finite and precious resource. Balancing the demands of a side hustle with existing commitments requires a mastery of time management—an art that holds the key to harmonizing personal, professional, and entrepreneurial pursuits. This chapter delves into the techniques that empower side hustlers to optimize their productivity, overcome time-related challenges, and find equilibrium amidst a bustling life.

The Essence of Time Management

Effective time management is not about squeezing more tasks into a day; it's about allocating time to activities that align with your priorities and goals. For side hustlers, this means ensuring that your entrepreneurial endeavors coexist harmoniously with your day job, family responsibilities, and personal well-being.

Begin by assessing your current time allocation. Track your activities over a week to identify patterns, time sinks, and areas where efficiency can be improved. This insight forms the foundation for crafting a personalized time management strategy.

Prioritization and Focus

The cornerstone of successful time management lies in prioritization. Identify the most critical tasks that contribute to your side hustle's growth and your overall well-being. The Eisenhower Matrix, a tool that categorizes tasks based on urgency and importance, can help you allocate your time effectively.

Embrace the power of deep work—a state of focused concentration that yields higher quality output in less time. Minimize distractions by setting dedicated work blocks, turning off notifications, and creating a clutter-free workspace. The Pomodoro Technique, which involves working in short, focused bursts followed by brief breaks, can enhance productivity and prevent burnout.

Managing Energy, Not Just Time

Time management is not solely about managing hours—it's also about managing your energy. Recognize when you're most energized and focused during the day, and schedule your most important tasks during these peak periods. For some, early mornings are optimal, while others find their flow in the afternoon or evening.

Regular breaks are vital for maintaining sustainable energy levels. Incorporate short walks, stretching, or mindfulness exercises to recharge and prevent mental fatigue. Prioritize self-care, as a well-rested and nourished mind is more productive and creative.

Overcoming Time-Related Challenges

Side hustlers often grapple with common time-related challenges, such as multitasking and overcommitting. Multitasking can lead to reduced productivity and increased stress. Instead, practice mono-tasking—focusing on one task at a time. Allocate specific time blocks for different tasks to maintain focus and minimize cognitive overload.

Overcommitting is a pitfall that can lead to burnout. Be honest with yourself about your capacity and learn to say no to commitments that don't align with your priorities. Delegate tasks when possible, and recognize that the pursuit of balance requires setting healthy boundaries.

Case Study: A Balanced Time Management Strategy

To illustrate effective time management, let's examine the case of David, a software developer with a passion for app development.

Prioritization and Focus: David uses the Eisenhower Matrix to categorize tasks for his side hustle. He dedicates his most productive hours—early mornings—to app development. He adopts the Pomodoro Technique, working in focused 25-minute intervals followed by a 5-minute break.

Managing Energy, Not Just Time: David recognizes that his creativity peaks in the afternoon. He uses this time for brainstorming and idea generation. He incorporates short walks during breaks to refresh his mind.

Overcoming Time-Related Challenges: David is committed to maintaining a healthy work-life balance. He declines non-essential commitments that could strain his schedule. He delegates some coding tasks to a trusted collaborator, freeing up his time for strategic planning.

Conclusion: Achieving Harmony Through Time Mastery

Balancing a side hustle with other commitments is a nuanced endeavor that demands skillful time management. By prioritizing tasks, embracing focus, and harnessing peak energy levels, side hustlers can optimize productivity and maintain their well-being. Overcoming common time-related challenges involves setting boundaries and practicing mono-tasking.

The case study of David serves as a testament to the effectiveness of these strategies. As you embark on your own journey of time mastery, remember that achieving balance is a dynamic process. Regular self-assessment, adaptation, and a commitment to self-care are essential for sustaining equilibrium.

In the grand symphony of life, mastering time management enables you to conduct each instrument—the side hustle, the day job, and personal passions—in harmonious synchronization. As you hone these skills, you not only elevate your productivity but also cultivate a fulfilling and purpose-driven existence. With a well-tuned sense of time, you're equipped to navigate the labyrinth of commitments and aspirations with grace and efficiency, achieving a true equilibrium that enriches every facet of your life.

CHAPTER SIX

Marketing Magic: Illuminating Your Side Hustle's Potential

In the bustling realm of side hustles, where resources are often limited, the art of marketing takes on a special significance. This chapter is your guide to unlocking marketing strategies tailored for side hustlers aiming to make a big impact on a limited budget. We'll traverse the landscape of social media, content creation, and networking, all essential avenues for attracting customers and building a loyal following. Additionally, we'll delve into the transformative power of storytelling and authentic branding, demonstrating how these elements can create a magnetic pull that sets your side hustle apart in a competitive market.

Strategic Marketing on a Limited Budget

Effective marketing doesn't require deep pockets—it requires creativity, authenticity, and a deep understanding of your target audience. Begin by defining your unique selling proposition (USP)—the element that sets your side hustle apart. This could be the quality of your product, exceptional customer service, or a compelling mission.

Leverage the power of digital marketing, which often presents cost-effective opportunities. Social media, content marketing, and community engagement are accessible avenues that allow you to connect directly with potential customers.

Harnessing the Potential of Social Media

Social media platforms are a treasure trove for side hustlers seeking to reach a wide and engaged audience. Begin by selecting the platforms that align with your target demographic. Each platform offers unique features and user behaviors, so tailor your content to suit each platform's nuances.

Engaging content is key to attracting and retaining followers. Share a mix of product highlights, behind-the-scenes glimpses, customer testimonials, and valuable information related to your niche. Consistency is crucial—maintain a regular posting schedule to remain on your audience's radar.

Crafting Compelling Content

Content creation is an invaluable tool for establishing your expertise and building trust with your audience. Start by identifying the type of content that resonates with your target audience. This could include blog posts, videos, infographics, or podcasts.

Content should offer value, whether it's entertainment, education, or inspiration. Address common pain points, share expert insights, or provide practical tips that align with your side hustle's niche. Engage with your audience by encouraging comments, questions, and discussions.

Networking: The Art of Building Relationships

Networking is a powerful strategy for side hustlers to expand their reach and create mutually beneficial relationships. Attend industry events, workshops, and meetups to connect with potential customers, collaborators, and mentors.

Online networking is equally impactful. Engage in relevant online communities, participate in discussions, and offer valuable insights. Building authentic connections lays the foundation for word-of-mouth marketing and organic growth.

The Power of Storytelling and Authentic Branding

Storytelling is a timeless technique that forms emotional connections between your side hustle and your audience. Share your journey, challenges, and triumphs—these narratives humanize your brand and allow customers to relate on a personal level.

Authentic branding goes hand in hand with storytelling. Consistent visual elements, a cohesive brand voice, and a genuine representation of your values create a brand identity that resonates. People are drawn to authenticity—your side hustle's story and values can become a compelling magnet for customers.

Case Study: Elevating a Side Hustle Through Strategic Marketing

Let's examine the case of Mia, a jewelry designer running a side hustle offering handcrafted artisanal jewelry.

Strategic Marketing on a Limited Budget: Mia defines her USP—her jewelry is not only visually stunning but also ethically sourced and environmentally conscious. She focuses on digital marketing to maximize her limited budget.

Harnessing the Potential of Social Media: Mia identifies Instagram and Pinterest as platforms suited for visual content. She posts high-quality images of her jewelry, showcasing the craftsmanship and sharing the stories behind each piece.

Crafting Compelling Content: Mia starts a blog where she shares articles about jewelry trends, care tips, and sustainable practices. She also creates short video tutorials demonstrating how customers can style her pieces.

Networking: The Art of Building Relationships: Mia attends local craft fairs and artisan markets, where she interacts directly with customers and fellow artisans. She also joins online jewelry-making forums and engages in discussions.

The Power of Storytelling and Authentic Branding: Mia shares her journey as a jewelry designer, her passion for sustainability, and her commitment to supporting ethical practices. Her branding reflects these values, creating a cohesive and authentic identity.

Conclusion: Igniting Your Side Hustle's Marketing Magic

Marketing, far from being a daunting task, is a canvas for creative expression and connection. On a limited budget, side hustlers can leverage strategic approaches that resonate with their target audience.

Social media, content creation, and networking provide accessible channels for engagement and growth.

However, the true magic lies in storytelling and authentic branding. Crafting narratives that embody your journey, values, and mission can ignite an emotional connection with customers. Your side hustle becomes more than a product—it becomes a story worth sharing, a brand worth believing in.

As you embark on your marketing journey, remember that authenticity is your most potent tool. Building genuine connections, delivering value, and staying true to your brand identity will establish your side hustle as a beacon in the crowded market. The strategies explored in this chapter empower you to create a marketing magic that not only attracts customers but also creates a lasting impact that transcends transactions, turning casual observers into passionate advocates of your side hustle's vision and purpose.

CHAPTER SEVEN

Scaling Up: Transitioning Your Side Hustle to a Thriving Enterprise

The journey from a fledgling side hustle to a full-fledged business is a transformative leap that requires careful planning, strategic decisions, and a bold vision. This chapter serves as your guide to scaling up, exploring avenues for growth, funding options, hiring strategies, and the art of managing expansion. Through inspiring stories of individuals who successfully transitioned their side hustles into their main source of income, you'll gain insights into the challenges and triumphs that accompany this exciting phase of entrepreneurship.

Unveiling Avenues for Expansion

Scaling up your side hustle is about envisioning its potential beyond its current boundaries. It involves capitalizing on the foundation you've built, exploring new markets, and diversifying your offerings.

Begin by assessing the scalability of your side hustle. Consider whether your current operations can handle increased demand, and identify areas where improvements are necessary. Research your target market to understand their evolving needs and preferences, allowing you to tailor your expansion strategy accordingly.

Funding Your Growth

Expanding your side hustle often requires additional resources, and securing funding is a pivotal step in this journey. Funding options range from personal savings and bootstrapping to external sources such as loans, grants, investors, and crowdfunding.

Before pursuing funding, create a comprehensive business plan that outlines your growth strategy, revenue projections, and potential return on investment. This plan serves as a blueprint for potential investors, demonstrating the viability of your expansion plans.

Hiring Your First Team Members

As your side hustle evolves, you may find yourself stretched thin. Hiring your first team members is a milestone that brings both relief and new challenges. Start by identifying roles that are crucial for maintaining and growing your business. Consider outsourcing tasks that fall outside your expertise to professionals who can help you streamline operations.

The hiring process involves writing compelling job descriptions, conducting interviews, and assessing candidates for their skills and cultural fit. Remember that building a strong team is instrumental in achieving your expansion goals.

Navigating Growth and Managing Challenges

Scaling up comes with a set of challenges that require adept management. Maintaining the quality of your products or services while meeting increased demand is a common hurdle. Implement systems and processes that ensure consistency and efficiency as your business grows.

Communication is paramount during this phase. Regularly update your customers on changes, improvements, and new offerings. Be transparent about any potential delays or adjustments to maintain trust.

Case Study: Transitioning From Side Hustle to Main Hustle

Let's delve into the story of Alex, a graphic designer who successfully transitioned his freelance design side hustle into a thriving design agency.

Unveiling Avenues for Expansion: After building a strong client base, Alex identified an opportunity to expand into offering branding and marketing services. He researched market trends and the needs of his existing clients, tailoring his expansion to meet their growing demands.

Funding Your Growth: Alex secured a business loan based on his comprehensive business plan, which projected increased revenue and ROI. The loan provided the capital needed to hire additional designers, invest in marketing efforts, and upgrade software and equipment.

Hiring Your First Team Members: Recognizing the need for specialized skills, Alex hired graphic designers, marketers, and an administrative assistant. He focused on hiring individuals who shared his vision and values, fostering a collaborative and innovative work environment.

Navigating Growth and Managing Challenges: As his agency expanded, Alex implemented project management software to streamline workflows and ensure timely delivery of projects. He maintained open lines of communication with clients, providing regular updates and seeking feedback.

Conclusion: Embracing Growth with Purpose and Strategy

Scaling up your side hustle is a transformative journey that requires a delicate balance of vision, strategy, and adaptability. As you chart the course from a side endeavor to a thriving enterprise, remember that growth should be purpose-driven.

Each decision—from funding to hiring to managing challenges—should align with your overarching goals and values. The stories of successful transitions inspire us to approach this phase with confidence, while also acknowledging that every journey is unique.

Embrace expansion as an opportunity to realize your entrepreneurial vision on a grander scale. With a strategic approach and an unwavering commitment to excellence, you can transition your side hustle into your main hustle, building a legacy that reflects your passion, dedication, and determination to create a meaningful impact in the world of business.